HANK
THE HEART

Written by:

Dr. Ryan A. Moore & Dr. John Hutton

Illustrated by:

Jeff Cimprich

Cat Musgrove

&Matt Nelson

Text copyright 2020 by Dr. Ryan A. Moore & Dr. John Hutton
Illustrations copyright 2020 by Jeff Cimprich, Cat Musgrove, & Matt Nelson

Published by blue manatee press, Cincinnati, Ohio.
blue manatee press and associated logo
are registered trademarks of Arete Ventures, LLC.

First Edition: February 2020.

Library of Congress Cataloging-In-Publication Data
Hank the Heart / by Dr. Ryan A. Moore and Dr. John Hutton; Illustrated by Jeff Cimprich, Cat Musgrove, and Matt Nelson—1st ed.
    Summary: Hank's a real heart, not like a Valentine—but he's the most lovable friend you'll ever find! Children will have fun getting to know Hank, as he leads them on an amazing tour of...himself! They'll learn what Hank's made of, how he works, how to keep him healthy, how doctors and nurses learn about him, and heart differences that children can be born with.
ISBN-13 (hardcover): 978-1-936669-78-3
[1. Juvenile Nonfiction – Concepts/Body. 2. Juvenile Nonfiction – Health & Daily Living/General.]
Printed in the USA.

Artwork was created digitally.

To Sandy, Blythe, Astrid and Clo - four
amazing chambers of my heart.
-Dr. John Hutton

To my three hearts that beat as one - Michelle,
Laney, and Dez - and to all the families with congenital heart
differences across the world!
-Dr. Ryan A. Moore

To my wife, Jessica, and my two children,
Ellie and Owen.
-Jeff Cimprich

To Brendan, Hank's number one fan!
-Cat Musgrove

To my Aunt Sue, for always encouraging my
art and helping me read.
-Matt Nelson

Special thanks to Dr. Ken Tegtmeyer for bringing us all together!

Let's learn about our bodies.

They're amazing! Where to start?

Let's look inside and say "Hello!"
to Hank the Heart!

Real hearts are kind of blobby, not like a Valentine.

Some say Valentine's hearts get their shape from leaves and seeds given as a sign of LOVE a long time ago!

But Hank's the most lovable friend that you'll ever find.

Made of **cardiac muscle** and oh so very strong,

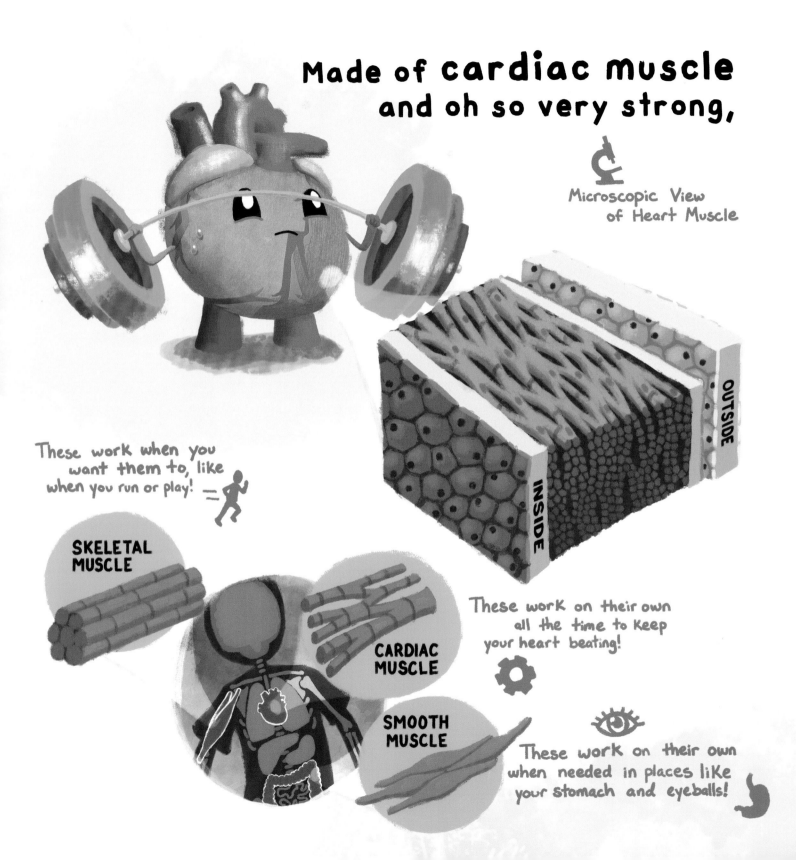

Microscopic View of Heart Muscle

INSIDE

OUTSIDE

These work when you want them to, like when you run or play!

SKELETAL MUSCLE

CARDIAC MUSCLE

These work on their own all the time to keep your heart beating!

SMOOTH MUSCLE

These work on their own when needed in places like your stomach and eyeballs!

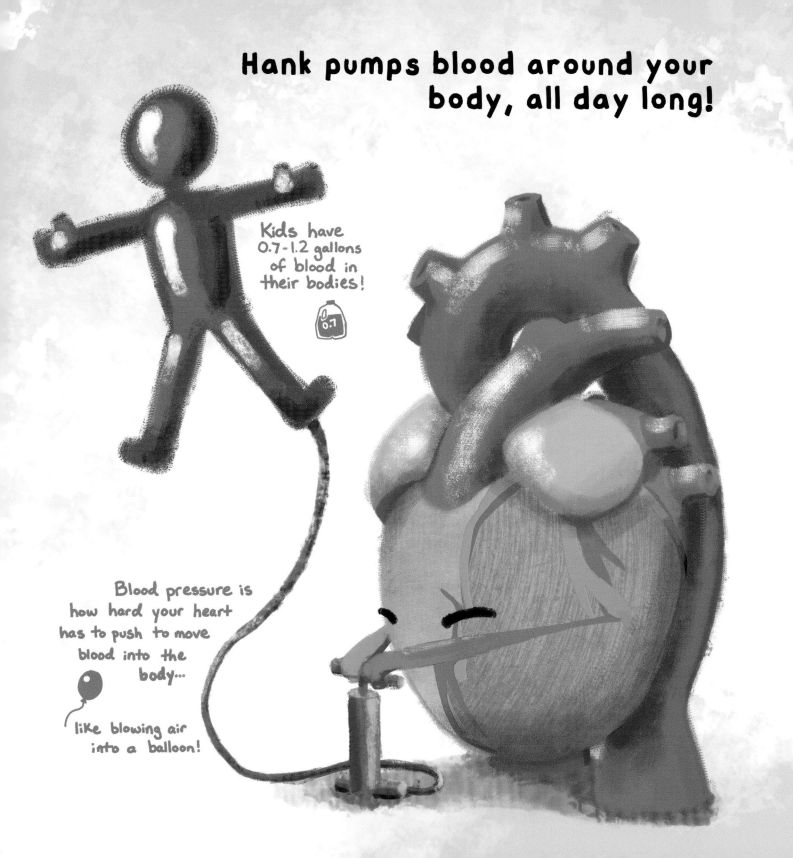

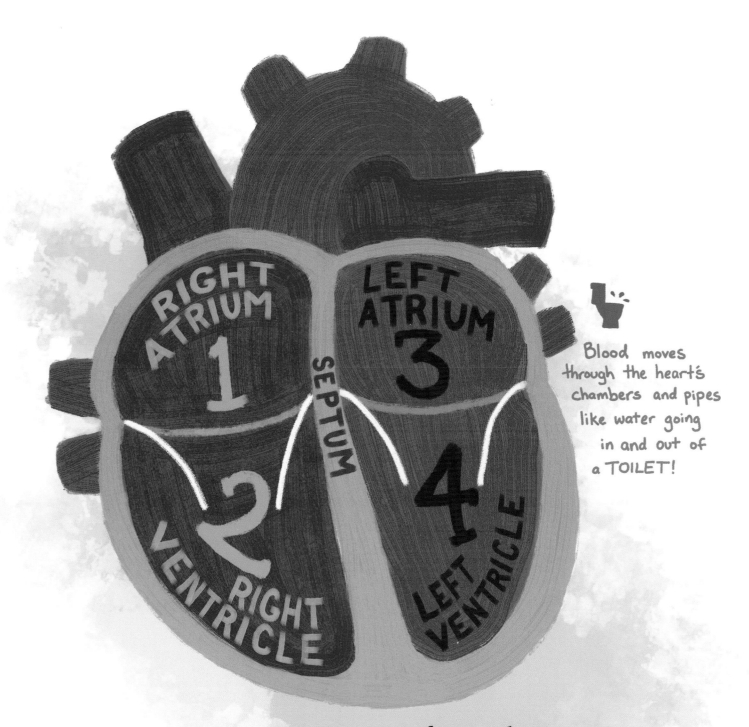

RIGHT ATRIUM 1

LEFT ATRIUM 3

SEPTUM

RIGHT VENTRICLE 2

LEFT VENTRICLE 4

Blood moves through the heart's chambers and pipes like water going in and out of a TOILET!

attached to four chambers of two very different types.

Between chambers are
valves, which are fantastic flaps.

When they're open, blood
flows through,

Closed Pulmonary Valve

Open Tricuspid Valve

Open Mitral Valve

Closed Aortic Valve

DIASTOLE

DIASTOLE ("Dye-as-ta-lee")
means RELAXING - it's when the
heart relaxes to fill with blood!

Tired blood fills Hank's right side:
It's blue* and needs air!

FROM THE BODY

OXYGEN is what we use from the air!

TO THE LUNGS

RIGHT VENTRICLE

LEFT VENTRICLE

FROM THE BODY

*Is tired BLOOD really BLUE? NO! Actually, blood with less oxygen is dark red!

VEINS carry blood back to the heart and look BLUE through your skin!

To the lungs! His **right ventricle** pumps it up there.

Red blood cells

LESS oxygen!

LOTS of oxygen!

RIGHT LUNG

LEFT LUNG

HANK LIVES HERE

Back from the lungs to Hank's left side: Red blood, there it goes!

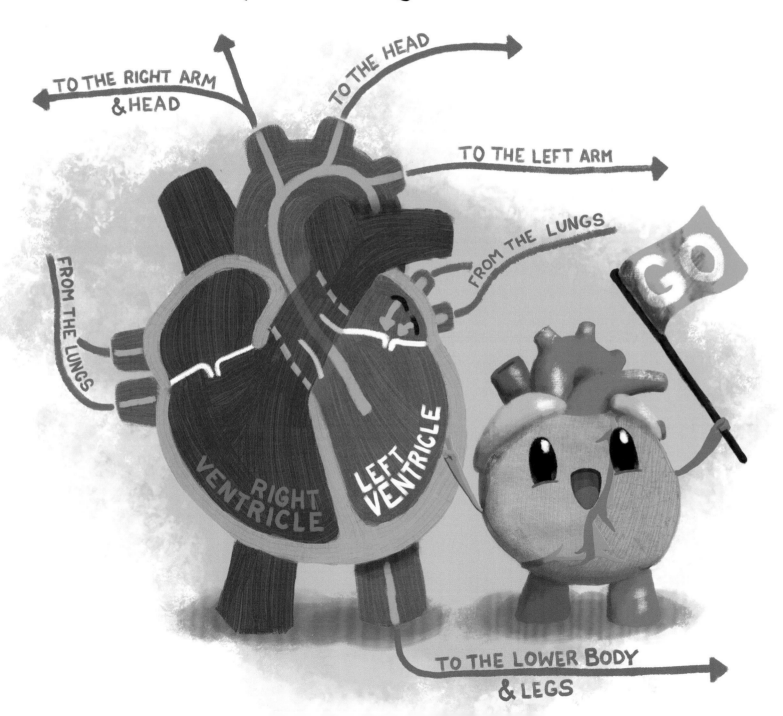

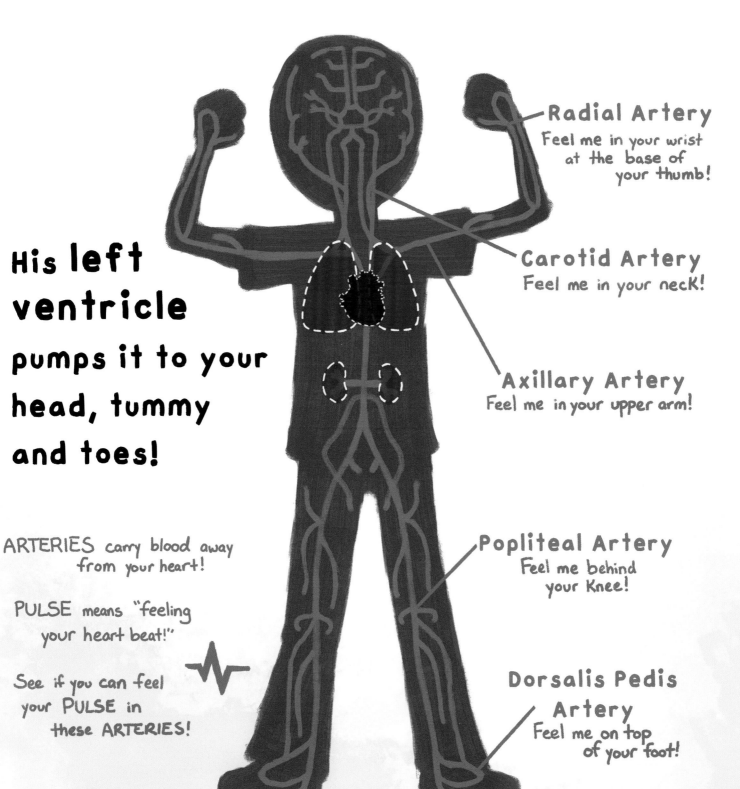

His left ventricle pumps it to your head, tummy and toes!

ARTERIES carry blood away from your heart!

PULSE means "feeling your heart beat!"

See if you can feel your PULSE in these ARTERIES!

Radial Artery
Feel me in your wrist at the base of your thumb!

Carotid Artery
Feel me in your neck!

Axillary Artery
Feel me in your upper arm!

Popliteal Artery
Feel me behind your knee!

Dorsalis Pedis Artery
Feel me on top of your foot!

To pump day and night, Hank's got his own coronary supply.

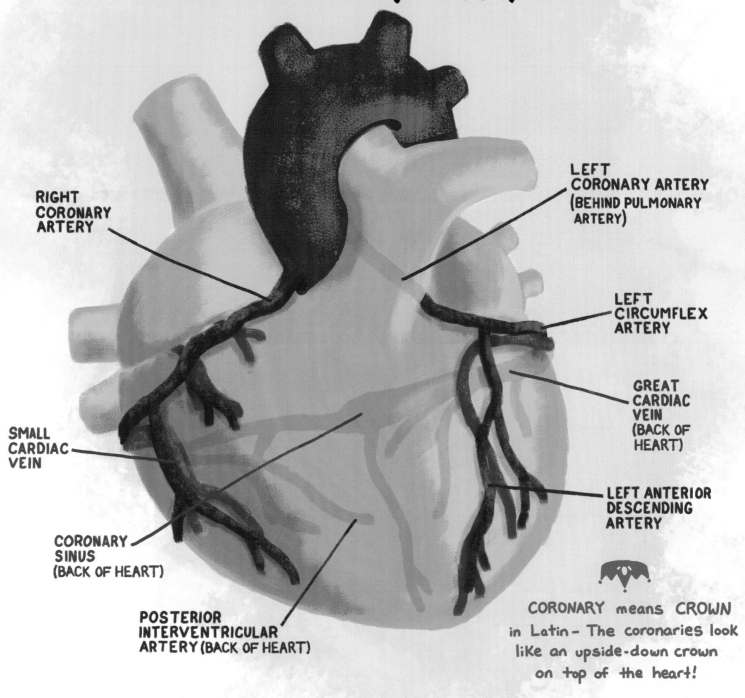

RIGHT CORONARY ARTERY

LEFT CORONARY ARTERY (BEHIND PULMONARY ARTERY)

LEFT CIRCUMFLEX ARTERY

GREAT CARDIAC VEIN (BACK OF HEART)

SMALL CARDIAC VEIN

CORONARY SINUS (BACK OF HEART)

LEFT ANTERIOR DESCENDING ARTERY

POSTERIOR INTERVENTRICULAR ARTERY (BACK OF HEART)

CORONARY means CROWN in Latin - The coronaries look like an upside-down crown on top of the heart!

Eat right and GO GO GO!
to keep his pumping power high.

Hank says, "Live 5-1-1-0!"

5 5 or more veggies and fruits per day!

No more than 1 hour of screen time per day!

1 1 hour or more of physical activity per day!

0 No sugary drinks!

Pumping slowly when you're sleeping,

and fast when you're at play;

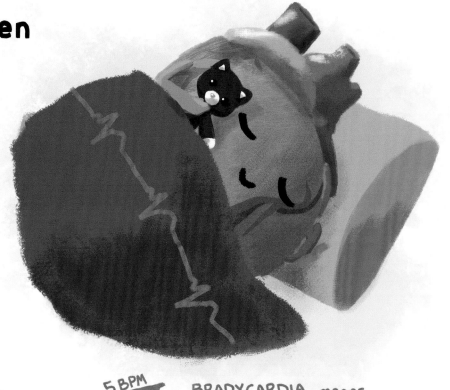

5 BPM BRADYCARDIA means SLOW HEART RATE.

The blue whale has one of the slowest at only 5 beats per minute!

85 BPM The normal human heart rate is between 60-110 beats per minute!

TACHYCARDIA means FAST HEART RATE.

1240 BPM The hummingbird has one of the fastest at 1,240 beats per minute!

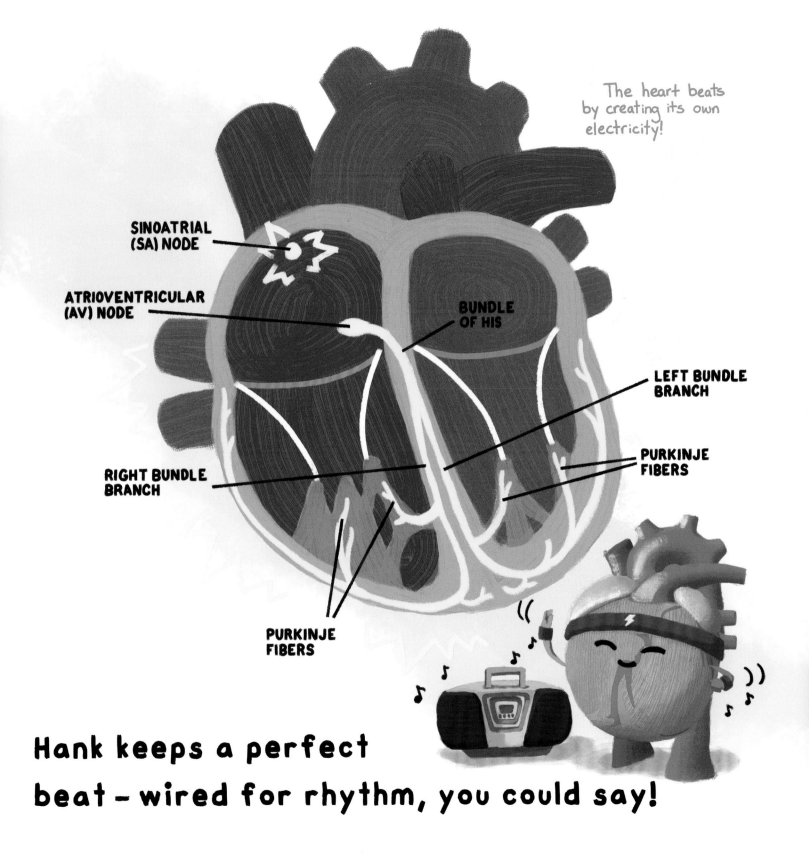

SINOATRIAL (SA) NODE

ATRIOVENTRICULAR (AV) NODE

BUNDLE OF HIS

LEFT BUNDLE BRANCH

RIGHT BUNDLE BRANCH

PURKINJE FIBERS

PURKINJE FIBERS

The heart beats by creating its own electricity!

Hank keeps a perfect beat - wired for rhythm, you could say!

Hank's sounds tell what he's doing: lub-dub, whoosh, rumble, burr-burr!

Normal Flow

Murmur Flow

*BURR-BURR isn't really a type of murmur- but it's a fun sound that rhymes!

When blood speeds up inside the heart, it's called a **murmur!**

A hand can feel Hank thumping, a **stethoscope** hears his sounds,

LUB-DUB!

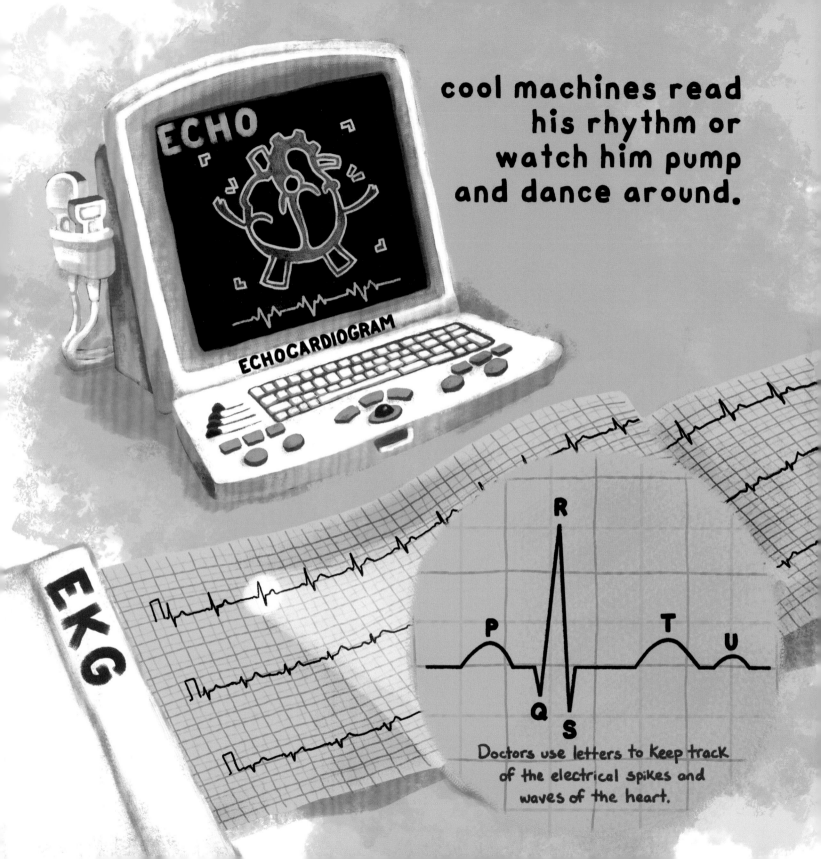

cool machines read his rhythm or watch him pump and dance around.

Hank's a medical marvel,
a complex construction indeed.

Some hearts are built differently, and a doctor's care they'll need.

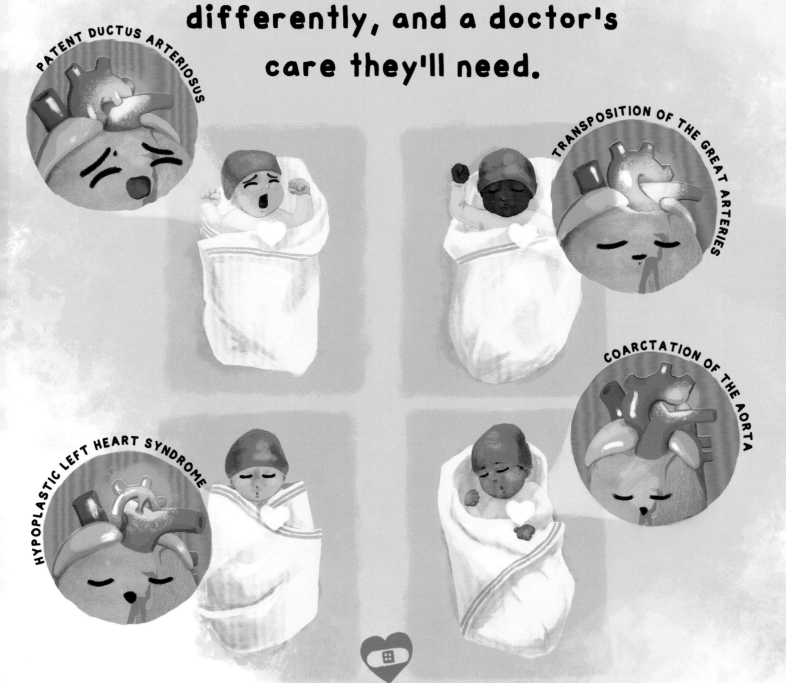

PATENT DUCTUS ARTERIOSUS

TRANSPOSITION OF THE GREAT ARTERIES

COARCTATION OF THE AORTA

HYPOPLASTIC LEFT HEART SYNDROME

CONGENITAL HEART DIFFERENCES are very common—they occur in 1 in 100 babies!

Chambers may need an extra boost, valves repaired and stitched.

Holes in walls may
need a patch,

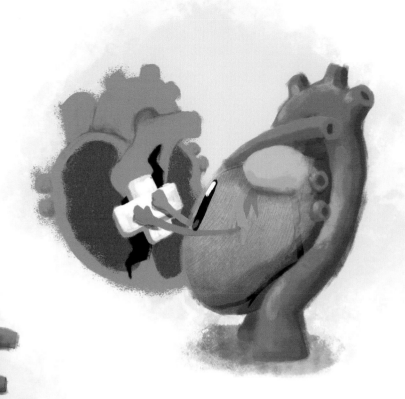

great vessels
to be switched.

HEART SURGEONS are
very skilled - they sew and come up
with creative ways to fix the heart!

No matter what, take care of Hank, be proud of who you are.

SCARS are a normal part of the skin's healing process – one on the chest from past heart surgery is called a STERNOTOMY SCAR.

Know that you are loved wholeheartedly,

on journeys near and far.

The heart helps us describe life's journey:

 "From the heart"- speaking and acting honestly.

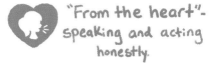 "Near one's heart"- loving those around you.

 "With all of my heart"- doing your best.

We've learned so much from our friend Hank,
but please take this to heart:

Have fun! Go play! Say "I love you"
-the most important part.

Glossary

DEOXYGENATED BLOOD: Blood which is low in oxygen and high in carbon dioxide.

OXYGENATED BLOOD: Blood which is high in oxygen and low in carbon dioxide.

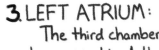

1. RIGHT ATRIUM: The first chamber to receive blood. Its job is to fill up with deoxygenated blood returning from the body.

3. LEFT ATRIUM: The third chamber to receive blood. Its job is to fill up with newly oxygenated blood returning from the lungs.

2. RIGHT VENTRICLE: The second chamber to receive blood. Its job is to pump deoxygenated blood to the lungs to get oxygen.

4. LEFT VENTRICLE: The fourth chamber to receive blood. Its job is to pump newly oxygenated blood to the body.

CHAMBERS: The four big rooms that make up the inside of the heart.

SYSTOLE: This is the part of the Cardiac Cycle when the heart pumps blood to the body – it has to SQUEEZE hard in order to do this!

DIASTOLE: This is the part of the Cardiac Cycle when the heart fills up with blood – it has to RELAX in order to do this!

CARDIAC CYCLE: This is the entire heart beat and includes time for filling and time for squeezing.

STETHOSCOPE: A medical instrument for listening to the heart.

ECHOCARDIOGRAM: A medical test that is able to see the heart using soundwaves – wait, what?! True! It transforms soundwaves into an image, kind of like how dolphins use echolocation to find fish!

HEART MURMUR: An extra noise that is heard when blood speeds up in the heart or in the vessels – sometimes it's related to heart differences, and sometimes it's just a harmless noise we hear.

ELECTRICAL SYSTEM OF THE HEART:

ELECTROCARDIOGRAM (EKG):

A medical test that records the electrical spikes and waves of the heart. Why PQRSTU? Some say it's because the inventor of the EKG, Dr. Einthoven, used "O" at the start and "X" at the end of each beat - and eventually filled out the middle with "PQRSTU"!

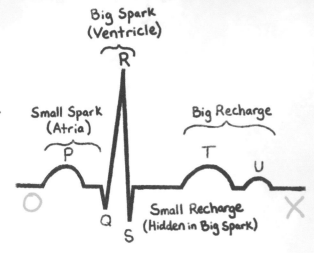

Big Spark (Ventricle)
R
Small Spark (Atria)
P
Big Recharge
T
U
O
Q
S
Small Recharge (Hidden in Big Spark)
X

1. SINOATRIAL (SA) NODE:

This special cluster of cells generates an electrical impulse to the atria that kicks off each beat! It's known as the "pacemaker" of the heart because it sets the "pace," or rate, of the heartbeat.

("purr-kin-gee")

5. PURKINJE FIBERS:

This is the last stop on the electrical train! These tiny fibers send the electricity directly to all cardiac muscle cells to make them beat together as one (we call it a "synchronized beat.")

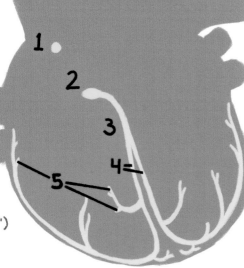

1
2
3
4 =
5

2. ATRIOVENTRICULAR (AV) NODE:

This cluster of cells receives electricity from the atria and pauses before passing it on to the rest of the electrical system.

This pause allows the heart to fill with blood before contracting. It also protects the heart from beating irregularly!

It's like the gatekeeper of the electrical system!

3. BUNDLE OF HIS:

No, "his" doesn't mean it's only found in boys! This bundle of cells was first described by a cardiologist named Dr. His.

It connects electricity from the AV Node to the ventricles via the Bundle Branches.

4. BUNDLE BRANCHES:

These branches send electricity to the left and right ventricles — like two big branches of a tree! When they get injured, they don't work as well - this is called "bundle branch block!"

Six Types of
Congenital Heart Differences
("Congenital" means "born with")

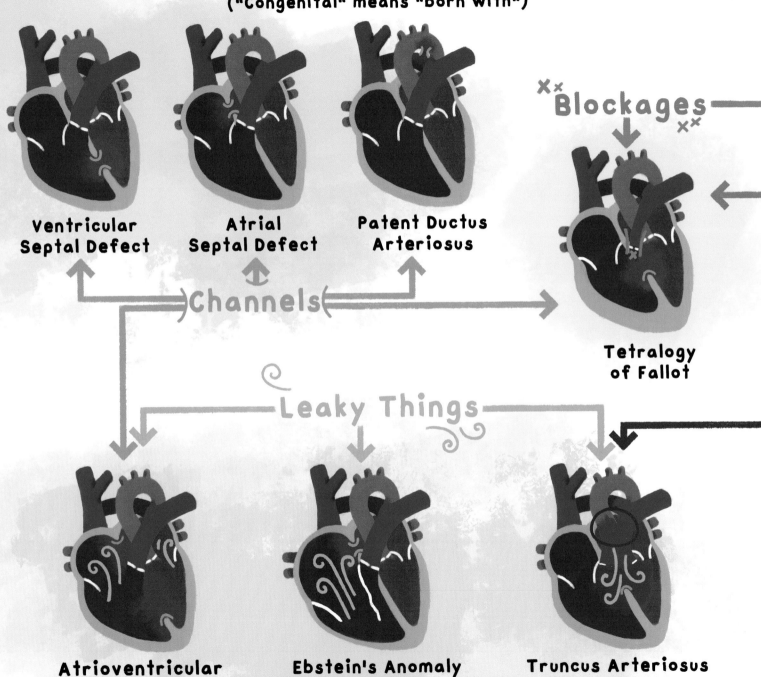

Ventricular
Septal Defect

Atrial
Septal Defect

Patent Ductus
Arteriosus

Blockages

Channels

Tetralogy
of Fallot

Leaky Things

Atrioventricular
Septal Defect

Ebstein's Anomaly

Truncus Arteriosus

Special thanks to Dr. Gil Wernovsky

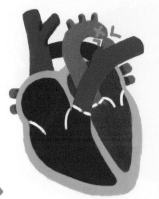

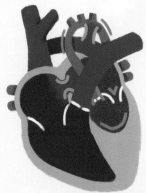

Coarctation of the Aorta

Hypoplastic Left Heart Syndrome

Small Things

)(Channels
✗ Blockages
↺ Leaky Things

— Small Things
∿ Missing Things
○ Mismatched Things

● Oxygenated Blood
● Mixed/Shunt Blood
● Deoxygenated Blood

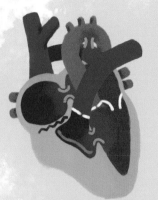

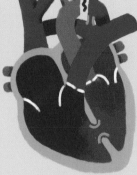

Tricuspid Atresia

Interrupted Aortic Arch

Missing Things

Mismatched Things

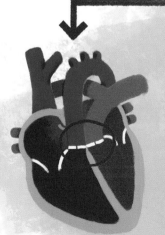

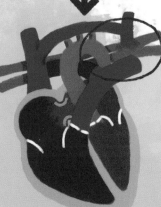

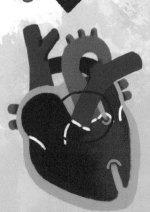

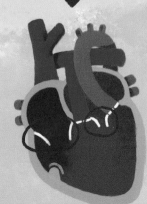

Transposition of the Great Arteries

Total Anomalous Pulmonary Venous Return

Double Outlet Right Ventricle

Double Inlet Left Ventricle

Diagram of the Heart

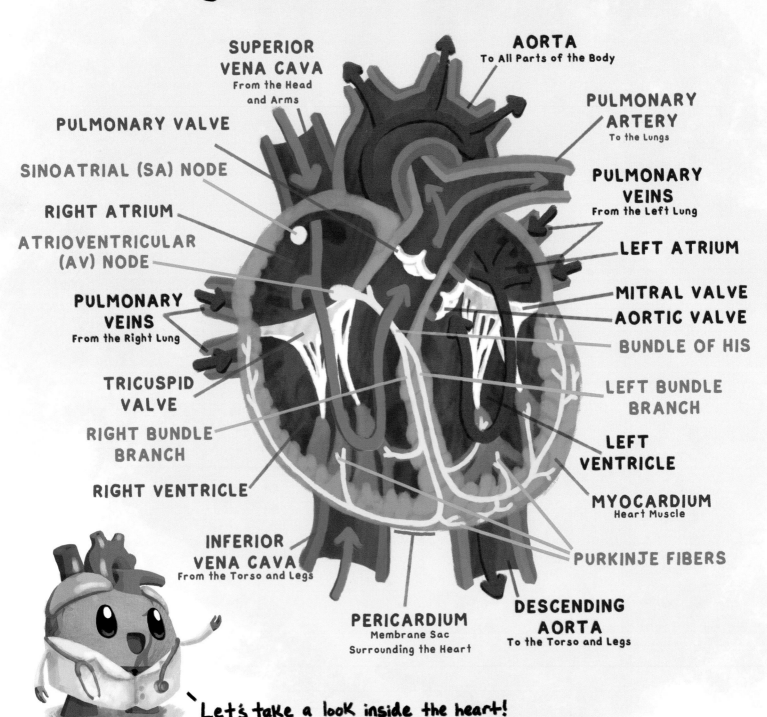

SUPERIOR
VENA CAVA
From the Head
and Arms

AORTA
To All Parts of the Body

PULMONARY VALVE

PULMONARY
ARTERY
To the Lungs

SINOATRIAL (SA) NODE

PULMONARY
VEINS
From the Left Lung

RIGHT ATRIUM

ATRIOVENTRICULAR
(AV) NODE

LEFT ATRIUM

PULMONARY
VEINS
From the Right Lung

MITRAL VALVE
AORTIC VALVE

BUNDLE OF HIS

TRICUSPID
VALVE

LEFT BUNDLE
BRANCH

RIGHT BUNDLE
BRANCH

LEFT
VENTRICLE

RIGHT VENTRICLE

MYOCARDIUM
Heart Muscle

INFERIOR
VENA CAVA
From the Torso and Legs

PURKINJE FIBERS

PERICARDIUM
Membrane Sac
Surrounding the Heart

DESCENDING
AORTA
To the Torso and Legs

Let's take a look inside the heart!

Resources

Special Resources for More Heart Information!

American Heart Association - www.heart.org

CardioSmart from the American College of Cardiology - www.cardiosmart.org

Cincinnati Children's Heart Encyclopedia and Heartpedia App - www.cincinnatichildrens.org/heartpedia

Heart University - www.heartuniversity.org

Johns Hopkins University/Cove Point Foundation - www.pted.org

...and many more! Check your local Children's Hospital site for other great materials on Congenital Heart Differences!

Some Organizations for Families with Congenital Heart Differences

Adult Congenital Heart Association - www.achaheart.org

Children's Heart Association of Cincinnati - www.chaoc.org

Mended Little Hearts - www.mendedhearts.org

National Pediatric Cardiology Quality Improvement Collaborative - www.npcqic.org

Pediatric Congenital Heart Association - www.conqueringchd.org

...and many more! Check your local area for other organizations supporting families with Congenital Heart Differences!

The End